Oxford Centre for the Mind

Visualisation

The Oxford Centre for the Mind:

Short Courses

Gary Lorrison

Visualisation

The Oxford Centre for the Mind

Short Courses

Powerful techniques to help you use your visual imagination to unleash the power of your mind.

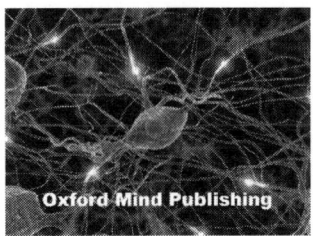

Gary Lorrison

Oxford Mind Publishing

THE OXFORD CENTRE FOR THE MIND LIMITED

#123,

94, London Road

Headington

Oxford OX3 9FN

email: info@oxfordmind.co.uk

web: www.oxfordmind.co.uk

Copyright ©2014 Gary Lorrison

All rights reserved. No portion of this publication may be reproduced, stored in a retrieval system, or transmitted in any form or by any means – electronic, mechanical, photocopy, recording, scanning, or other – except for brief quotations in critical reviews or articles, without the prior written consent of the publisher.

Oxford Mind Publishing is a division of the Oxford Centre for the Mind Limited.

ISBN-13:
978-1499660746

ISBN-10:
149966074X

About the Author

Having studied law at Cambridge, Gary Lorrison started off his career working in London as a solicitor but quickly saw the light and left the legal profession to develop his interest in the mind. He quickly earned two degrees in philosophy but found himself focusing on how one could use the techniques of philosophy, psychology and science to run one's mind more effectively.

Since 2003, he has been actively involved in running personal development training programmes to help people improve their mental performance. He has a special interest in memory training and other ways of helping people absorb information as well as the techniques of logical, critical and analytical thinking and the limits of human rationality.

In his spare time he enjoys walking in the countryside, takes a keen interest in music playing a number of instruments and is an occasional skydiver.

He lives on a farm near Oxford with four dogs, three cats, three ducks, six geese, about five hundred sheep and the occasional human being.

Testimonials

Testimonials for our seminars: -

"Excellent - best course I have been on in ages - thought provoking and insightful"

"Great workshop. Coach created a very relaxing, easy and open atmosphere. Coach was helpful and had a very pleasant way of interacting with us"

"I am very happy I came to this workshop. It was good value for money and provided very useful skills that I know will help my studies"

"It's a great course - I would recommend you go on it"

"Good fun and value for money"

"Do it! - Very interesting and a good approach to de-stressing about work levels etc."

"It really works, especially the visualisation techniques"

For information on all of the courses run by the Oxford Centre for the Mind please visit our website:

www.oxfordmind.co.uk

Visualisation

Contents

1. Introduction — 9
2. What is Visualisation — 10
3. Practical Visualisation — 16
4. Developing your Senses — 32
5. Ongoing Practice — 37
6. Endword — 41
7. Visualisation Materials — 42

Visualisation

ONE

INTRODUCTION

Aims

The aim of the *Visualisation Course* is to explain to you what visualisation is and why it is an important mental skill to develop. It will provide you with a number of exercises to help you develop your own visualisation skills and show you how the ability to visualise applies to other aspects of our courses.

This course is divided into two sections. The first deals with introducing you to visualisation and gives you various strategies for developing your visualisation skills. The second part concentrates on developing your five main external senses – sight, hearing, smell, taste and touch. Developing these is an integral part of developing your visualisation skills, and will give you a greater appreciation of the outside world in general.

Like the *Concentration and Focus Course*, this course provides a strong foundation for many of the other courses in mental and cognitive development, and therefore you should give it the attention it deserves, even if some of the ideas initially may seem a little unfamiliar to you.

Practical nature of the course

Remember as you go through this course that it is designed to be practical, not theoretical. You should do all of the exercises when we indicate. If you just read through the course without doing these exercises, you might gain an intellectual understanding of what the course is about, but you will not gain the benefits you will from actually doing the exercises.

TWO

WHAT IS VISUALISATION?

Visualisation is simply the use of the imagination to make mental pictures, sounds, smells, tastes or feelings. It involves using your mind's eye to see, rather than your actual eyes; rather than using your ears to hear, it involves using your *mind's ear*, and so on with the other senses. This is an ability that most of us possess to a greater or lesser degree, but it is a skill that is often underdeveloped, and improving one's ability to visualise can have a number of significant benefits.

The word visualisation implies that it is primarily a visual skill, and for most people this is indeed the case. For example, the majority of people find it is easier to imagine pictures than smells. However, the term *visualisation* includes all five senses (sight, hearing, smell, taste and touch) and fully developing one's visualisation skills involves developing the ability to imagine in all five senses. Given this, it might be more accurate to call this course *sensualisation* rather than *visualisation*, but since the word *visualisation* is well established, we will continue to use it here.

Why develop your ability to visualise?

Our physiology and neurology respond in the same or similar ways for an internal stimulus as they do for an external stimulus. An internal stimulus is something that we imagine is happening to us, while an external stimulus is something that actually does happen to us. What this means is that our bodies and brains respond in the same way when we vividly imagine something as they do when we actually experience it.

An example of this is the *placebo effect* in medicine. The placebo effect occurs when a patient believes that he is receiving treatment, but the treatment is in fact, unknown to him, completely ineffective. The patient's belief that he is receiving proper treatment leads to an improvement in his condition.

This has practical consequences for the medical establishment. When a new drug is being tested, some of the test subjects will be given the real drug, while some will be given a treatment designed to look like the real thing which has no effect at all: a placebo. For the new drug to be considered effective, it must produce an effect greater than the placebo.

In the field of education, the results a student obtains can be affected by their teacher's expectations of them. If a teacher is told that a student is particularly bright compared to the average, his or her results are likely to be better than average, even if he or she is in fact just an average student. Similarly, if the teacher is told that a student is dim, even if it is not true, he or she will tend to receive lower marks. This occurs because the teacher's beliefs and expectations influence how he perceives the two students' abilities, and thus influences him in his dealings with them.

In the wild, if one animal is being chased by another, it releases adrenalin into its bloodstream which enables it to run farther and faster than it normally could. At the stage that the adrenalin is released, it is unlikely that anything bad has actually happened to the animal: it is simply the anticipation of what might happen that causes the physiological response.

At a more trivial level, if someone drinks white wine that has, without their knowledge, been coloured red with a tasteless dye, it will taste like red wine to them, because that is what they expect to experience.

These examples serve to show that what is goes on in your imagination can be very important: just as important as what is actually happening to you. This is the case even if the use of your imagination is completely

Visualisation

unconscious. By transforming the use of your imagination from an unconscious to a conscious process, you can bring it under your control, use it to achieve specific outcomes in specific situations, and enhance its effectiveness. This course is designed to help you do just that.

For example, the power of visualisation can be used consciously to change how the body functions. It can be used to calm the body down, slow the heartbeat, alter the flow of blood round the body, and raise or lower body temperature.

By using visualisation techniques, people have succeeded in producing remarkable outcomes for themselves, from reducing pain and the effects of injury, to enhancing their memories, their ability to achieve their goals, their sporting capabilities and their physical capacities.

An example of the latter, if only anecdotal, is that of the mother who lifts a car off her injured child. Normally, of course, she would stand no chance of doing so. So how is it that she can in an emergency? The car is just as heavy. What has changed is her neurology. For her the world is different and she uses this fact to change how her body functions. The fact that there is an emergency causes adrenalin to be released into her bloodstream, enhancing her strength. But what causes the release of adrenalin in the first place is how she perceives the world. If she could learn to represent the world in exactly the same way using the power of her imagination, she would be lifting cars on a consistent basis!

Weightlifters often use precisely this technique to increase the number of times that they can lift a weight. When a weightlifter is tired out and thinks that he cannot lift a certain weight any more, he will often get a partner to help him with the lift, getting him to provide just enough assistance to enable him to lift the weight one more time. Often, however, the partner will not need to do any more than just look as if he is helping. The weightlifter's belief that he is receiving assistance is enough for him to manage to lift the weight once again.

Uses of visualisation
So how can you use visualisation to change your life? The previous examples show how you might be able to use it to achieve certain physical outcomes. There are many other areas where you can use it to make a difference.

Memory
You can use visualisation to help improve your memory. We develop these ideas further in our memory courses. Suffice to say for now that visual recognition memory has been shown to be essentially perfect, so developing your ability to picture events in your mind will help you to develop your memory. One of the exercises later in this course will help you use this ability to recall the events of every day of your life.

Achieving your goals in life
By developing your powers of visualisation, you can use your imagination to visualise your goals with real clarity and precision. You will learn to experience them as if they were real and as if they were happening now. This will help to give you an idea of exactly what it is that you want to achieve, what is important to you and what is not. It will also enable you to become emotionally involved with your goals, so you will feel what it is like to achieve them. Being able to access these feelings will help you to stay motivated, and to stay on the path to achieving them.

Achieving your physical goals
We have already shown how you can use visualisation to improve your physical performance. You can use this knowledge to improve your results in any sport that you participate in: to run faster, lift heavier weights, improve your stamina and so on.

Visualisation

Sir Roger Bannister was the first person to run a four-minute mile. Before he did so he would visualise himself running the mile in less than four minutes. Until then, it had been thought to be impossible, but as soon as he achieved it, many other runners were able to manage it, showing that the limit was not a physiological limit, but rather a limit imposed by the power of people's beliefs. By using your imagination to change your perceptions you will be able to break through barriers you previously thought were impossible.

You can also use visualisation to practise sporting skills. In a study of basketball players, a group who visualised themselves practising, by imagining themselves shooting balls into a hoop, showed a similar improvement to a different group that actually practised. Such is the power of the mind.

Using visualisation to boost creativity

You can use the power of visualisation to boost your creativity. When you are visualising you are using your imagination, and the more you use your imagination, the more creative you will become. As with any skill, the more you practise it, the better you will become, so take this opportunity to develop your powers of visualisation to as high a level as you can.

Other uses of visualisation

The number of things that you can do using visualisation is essentially infinite. Anything that you can do in the real world, you can also imagine yourself doing. As you develop your visualisation skills your ability to imagine clearly and vividly will improve and so will your ability to replicate those results in the outside world. It is, then, a vitally important skill to develop.

Onword

In the following section we will provide you with the opportunity to find out how good your powers currently are, and give you a number of extended exercises that will help you to develop your abilities.

THREE

PRACTICAL VISUALISATION

In this section we are going to ask you to do an exercise to assess your initial powers of visualisation. You can come back to this exercise after a few months to see how your abilities have improved over time. After that, we set out a number of different visualisation exercises that will give you a chance to develop your own abilities further and overcome any difficulties you may have. We will also provide you with sufficient knowledge to enable to develop your own visualisation exercises.

Inability to visualise?

Before we start it is necessary to challenge a belief that some people have concerning visualisation, namely that they cannot visualise at all. Many people certainly believe that they cannot form any mental images. In fact, if this is true at all, it is true in only a tiny number of cases.

If you think that you fall into this category, it may be that you are forming mental images, but do not realise that you are. Try this exercise: attempt to visualise something very simple, like an apple. What colour is it? What shape is it? How big is it? If you can answer any of these questions then you are drawing on your visual memory of the object and if you can do that then you can visualise it. Your abilities may not be very well developed at present, but you do have the ability to visualise.

If you find forming primarily *visual* images to be a problem, try starting off by using a different sense to lead you into the visual image. For example, if you want to form a picture of a covering of snow on the ground but are having difficulty doing so, try using sound instead: imagine hearing a footfall in crunchy snow, and use that as trigger to help you form the visual image. Alternatively, you could use smell: if you want to imagine what a rose looks like, start off by imagining how it smells, and use that to help you form the visual image.

If you think you have difficulty forming auditory images, try this exercise: without speaking out loud, in your head, complete the following quotes: -

"To be or not to be, ...", Hamlet;

"One for all, and ... ...", the Three Musketeers;

"Yesterday, all my troubles ... ...", the Beatles;

"Our Father, who art in Heaven, ...", the Lord's Prayer.

The answers are at the end of this chapter. If you were able to get the answers, then despite what you may think, you do have the ability to form auditory images. All you have to develop these abilities is to practise.

Assessing your powers of visualisation

Whatever you think about your powers of visualisation, we suggest that you try the following exercise, designed to assess your current abilities. This will give you a baseline to measure yourself against and you can return to this exercise when you have completed the course to see how you have improved.

Visualisation

You will be asked to create a number of different mental images. Give yourself a score for each one as follows: -

If you are not able to visualise anything, score 0

If you can visualise something but the image is not clear, score 1

If you can visualise something and the image is quite clear, score 2

If you can visualise a clear image, score 3

If you can visualise a very clear image, score 4

You will find that some of the following images focus more on one sense than on another, but try and visualise using all your senses if you can.

Primarily sight
1. Visualise the house you grew up in.
2. Visualise a close relative.
3. Visualise the eyes of a good friend looking worried.

Primarily hearing
4. Imagine you are listening to the first few bars of a favourite song.
5. Imagine the sound of an aircraft taking off.
6. Imagine the sound of a famous person giving a speech.

Primarily smell
7. Imagine the smell of lavender.
8. Imagine the smell of freshly cut grass.
9. Imagine the smell of oranges.

Primarily taste
10. Imagine the taste of your favourite dessert.

11   Imagine the taste of lemon juice.
12   Imagine the taste of toast.

Primarily kinaesthetic
13   Imagine the feeling of throwing a ball.
14   Imagine the rough feeling of sandpaper.
15   Imagine how it feels to lift a heavy object.

More than one sense
16   Imagine the look and feel of your favourite clothes.
17   Imagine relaxing on a beach on a South Sea Island.
18   Imagine a kettle boiling over.
19   Imagine riding a bicycle up a steep hill.
20   Imagine walking in a strong wind while it is raining.

When you have finished add up your score and make a note of it.

A score between 60 and 80 is very good.

A score between 30 and 60 is good but capable of improvement.

A score of less than 30 means that you would definitely benefit from some visualisation training as set out within this course.

Repeat this exercise after three months of visualisation training to see how your abilities have improved.

Preparing to visualise

You are now ready to move on to the exercises designed to develop your visualisation abilities. Before you start, it is important that you are properly prepared and in the right frame of mind, so please pay attention to the following factors: -

Time

You will need to set aside twenty to thirty minutes when you are unlikely to be disturbed by anyone else.

Environment

Choose a place to that is quiet, clean and pleasant. It should be somewhere that you will feel comfortable, that you will want to return to, and somewhere that you won't be disturbed.

If possible, use a separate room, or mark off a part of a room that you can devote solely to these exercises. You might wish to light scented candles. Do whatever it takes to create a pleasant atmosphere that works for you.

If you want to, you can do these exercises outside in the open air, provided that there are no distractions. If you live in the countryside or by the sea, or anywhere where there is a pleasant outdoor environment, this would be an excellent alternative.

Make sure that you do your exercises where it is not too bright. If you are indoors, shut the curtains, and dim the lights, although make sure that you have sufficient light to read by. If you are outside, try to choose a time of day when the sun is not too bright, or stay in the shade.

Your physical state

To gain best results, you should be free of all physical distractions: muscular tension, itches and so on. Any physical discomfort, tension or stress is likely to distract you and you should do whatever you can to reduce or eliminate it before you start.

Clothing

Make sure that you are wearing comfortable, warm, loose clothing: no shoes, but socks are okay. Make sure that you aren't wearing anything tight that is likely to cause discomfort, as you will be sitting still for some time.

You may wish to have a blanket handy as your body temperature is likely to drop as you relax.

Posture

We suggest that you do the visualisation exercises in either a sitting position or lying down.

If you are going to sit, you can either sit in a chair or on the floor. If you decide to use a chair, try and use one with a straight, hard back. This will help keep your back straight and prevent you from slouching. You knees should not be too bent - they should be at an angle greater than 90 degrees (that means that your feet should be further away than your knees from your chair). Rest your hands in your lap or wherever they feel most comfortable.

If you would rather sit on the floor, you can sit either cross-legged, or in the lotus position. If you find it difficult to sit like this, try sitting with your back against a wall or with a cushion under your backside. Again rest your hands in your lap in whatever way feels comfortable.

Whichever way you decide to sit, concentrate on keeping your back straight and your head well balanced. Make sure that you are sitting on your sitting bone, located under your buttocks, and not slouched at all. This will ensure that your body is balanced, that your muscles are relaxed and that any physical tension is minimised. You should be as comfortable as you possibly can.

Only lie down if you are having someone else read to you or if you are going to listen to the visualisation exercises on tape, not if you are going to read to yourself.

Diet
Make sure that you eat healthily before the first time you practise and avoid alcohol and any kind of drugs for twenty-four hours beforehand if at all possible. Avoid doing the visualisation exercises within one hour of eating.

Phone
Take the phone off the hook or turn it off, so that you will not be disturbed.

Family
Make sure your family or other household members know that you would like to have this period of time to yourself and do not want to be disturbed. If they want to join in with you, that is perfectly acceptable, and doing these exercises in a group can be fun.

Music
We suggest that initially, at least, you do these exercises in silence, just to get a sense of how it feels to do so. You may, though, eventually, want to do them with music or other relaxing sounds playing in the background. If you do the exercises in an outdoor environment, you may well hear some natural sounds such as birdsong, wind or animal noises anyway and you should not find these distracting.

If you do use your own music, make sure that what you choose is conducive to relaxation. Led Zeppelin's music may indeed be great, but it is unlikely to help your reach a relaxed state of mind!

Certain types of music are very good for helping still the mind, inducing an *alpha* state, and harmonizing mind and body. Classical music from the Baroque period, particularly Bach, is effective, as is music by Mozart, Telemann and Handel. The aim of the composers in this period was to create compositions of a harmonious whole, and the result of this is music which is ideal for achieving a relaxed state of mind. Alternatively, you might like to try Indian classical music, the aim of which is to encourage certain moods, or the sounds of waves breaking against a shore, or birdsong. In fact, you can use anything that helps you attain a relaxed state of mind without distracting you.

Timer

Initially, we suggest you do the exercises for no more than twenty minutes at a time. You may lose track of time while you are doing them, so make sure that you have some way of knowing when your time is up, such as an alarm clock. As you progress, you might like to extend the time that you spend in doing your visualisation exercises. You may find that when you have decided how long you want to spend visualising, your inner body clock will let you know when your time is up with a surprising degree of accuracy.

Paper and Pen

When you have finished, you might find it beneficial to make a note of your experiences and how the visualisations went for you, so have a pen and paper handy. You may want to use a notebook or journal so that you can keep all your notes together in one place.

Starting off
When you are ready to start, sit down in whichever manner you have chosen. Sit still for five minutes, and allow yourself to relax. Breathe deeply from your abdomen. Breathe in for a count of three, hold for another three count, and exhale for a count of three. Do not strain as you breathe. When you have spent five minutes sitting like this, breathing deeply and relaxing, you should be ready to start your chosen visualisation exercise. Command your mind to be still.

The visualisation exercises
Having prepared properly, you should now ready to begin. There are seven visualisations included in this course. These will provide you with enough experience to gain an understanding of what they involve and enable you to develop your own visualisations if you should want to. The purpose of these visualisations is to get you to use your imagination fully, using all five senses, so really try to ensure that you do this. The more you use all your different senses, the more you will get out of the exercises, and the more enjoyable you will find them.

Selecting the visualisation exercise
Now that you are ready to start, turn to the materials section and select the first visualisation entitled *Home Visualisation*. You can either read this to yourself or have someone else read it to you. If you read it to yourself, read through one paragraph at a time and do as asked before moving on to the next one. Take your time and be sure not to rush.

 If someone else is reading to you, they should speak slowly and clearly, in a calm monotone. There should be pauses after each sentence to allow you to really get a grip of the images before moving on. You might want to arrange a signal that you can give to your partner indicating when you would like them to pause, and when you would like them to move on. This way, you can ensure that your partner speaks at a pace preferable to you. Ideally, the signal should be non-verbal, such as a wave of the hand or something similar.

A further alternative is to record the visualisation exercise onto tape and play it back, as you sit relaxed with your eyes closed. You can then use the pause button to maintain control of the pace of the exercise. If you do choose to make a recording, speak slowly in a relaxed, calm, monotonous voice.

What you will experience

As you start you will probably notice that you become much more relaxed. You may notice your breathing slowing down, your body becoming heavier, and your body temperature falling. You may notice that your hands and feet start to feel heavy. This is natural and nothing to worry about. It merely indicates that you are indeed becoming very relaxed. Overall you should find the experience very enjoyable and relaxing.

If you are sufficiently relaxed, you might find that the visualisations are similar to a very pleasant dream, in which you experience events just as if you were really there. However, unlike dreams, you will be in control of what happens from beginning to end.

Visualising

Sit quietly and listen to or read the visualisation exercise. You will simply be asked to imagine seeing, hearing, smelling, tasting and touching certain different things in a particular environment. Get into the experience as much as you possibly can and really enjoy it. Make sure that you use *all* of your senses. This is very important – the more you can use all the different senses, the greater the benefits will be.

Visualisation

We have included seven different visualisations in this course. Some are more involved than others, but they are all designed to stimulate all five senses, so do try to ensure that all of your senses are engaged. Do not limit yourself precisely to the words on the page: let your imagination run free.

We have suggested that you do the *Home Visualisation* first as this has more sensory cues for you to latch on to than the others. In the subsequent exercises, you will have to use your imagination some more. In the initial stages, make sure that you limit yourself to one exercise per day.

Each visualisation exercise should take between ten and twenty minutes. Feel free to extend it if you are enjoying the experience and make sure you do not rush. The aim is to develop your internal senses and you will find this easier if you allow the experience to encompass you slowly.

Afterwards

When you have completed the visualisation exercise, take some time just to sit or lie down and relax. You should be feeling very relaxed by now anyway. After five minutes, gradually bring your focus back to the outside world, but try to stay in a relaxed state of mind.

At this point we suggest you make some notes of your experience.

Pay attention to the following factors: -

- Were you able to visualise strongly in all senses, or were some stronger or weaker than others? Give yourself a score using the same scoring system as you used for the exercise entitled '*Assessing your powers of visualisation*' on page 17.

- If you had difficulty with a particular sense, was it made better or worse by being associated with another sense? For instance, did a smell help to trigger a particular visual memory?

- How did the experience feel? Was it enjoyable? Or if it wasn't, why not?

- Did you notice any memories being triggered? Are you able to determine what it was that triggered them?

- For subsequent exercises assess whether you feel that your abilities are improving and what factors you think are affecting this.

Difficulties with visualising

You may encounter some of the following problems with visualisation: -

Difficulty Forming Images

The main difficulty that you will probably have is difficulty forming a mental image. We have already suggested one approach that you can take: you can use one sense stimulus such as smell, as a lead in to another such as sight.

Another thing you can do to counter this is make sure that you are sufficiently relaxed and free of anxieties. If you do, then the images will come. Pay attention to the advice in the preparation section and make sure that you are relaxed both mentally and physically, free of tension, and that your breathing is slow and deep.

If you feel anxious while doing the visualisation exercises, try and work out what the cause of the anxiety is. It may be physical. For instance, you may be physically tense and unable to relax. If so exercises such as yoga may help you to relax.

Deal with any other physical distractions as they occur, such as scratching an itch or blowing your nose. If you don't deal with them as they occur, they might end up becoming much more of a distraction.

Visualisation

It may be that you feel anxious for other reasons – work, financial, personal and so on. If that is the case and you really don't think that you will be able to concentrate on visualising, consider postponing the visualisation element of the exercises either until later on in the day or to the following day. However, persevere with the relaxation elements of the exercises, as they will help to reduce your anxiety.

Impatience

Another possible obstacle to success is impatience. If your ability to visualise is underdeveloped, it may take some time before you can do so to the degree you might wish. In our consumerist society we tend to want results quickly, and quite often will not tolerate anything that does not bring immediate results. You *will* notice changes in your ability to visualise if you practise consistently, but it may take some time, and, like the *Concentration & Focus Course*, the benefits are cumulative, so to gain the full benefits from this course you must persevere. We will say more about this in the *Ongoing Practice* section.

Continuing with the visualisation exercises

When you have done all seven exercises, you can either repeat them or start to develop your own. If you choose to develop your own try to emulate the ones that we have set out here. Make sure that the images are pleasant, the sort that you might want to return to and that they stimulate all of your senses. If you are developing your own, you can choose to make them as long as you want.

Make sure that you refer to the *Ongoing Practice* section. This will help you to get the best out of your exercises.

Using visualisation to enhance your performance

After you have been practising visualisation for some time your skills should be sufficiently developed to put them to some practical use. We are going to outline how you can use your visualisation skills to focus on three areas: memory, physical performance, and achieving your goals.

Memory

We will deal with using visualisation to enhance your memory in much more detail in our memory courses. The essential point, if you want to remember something, is to make a visual image of the item or items that you want to remember. So, say you want to remember a dog and a bicycle, make as vivid a mental image of the two as you possibly can. Make sure that you incorporate all five senses in the formation of the image, so imagine what the dog sounds like, how it feels, smells and so on. Do the same for the bike.

You can make the two items even more memorable by making them interact with each other. Rather than just visualising the dog and a bike separately, make them interact with each other. For example, you could visualise the dog riding the bike, or peeing on the bike.

You could also use visualisation as a means of recalling the events of your life. This is something you can do in bed at the end of the day. As you relax before going to sleep, conduct a mental review of the day's events by visualising the significant events of the day. As with all visualisation, make sure that you use all five senses. Since your imagination is more flexible than real life, you can review the events of the day much more quickly than it takes to experience them, so you can review a whole day's events in a few minutes.

If you decide to do this, make sure that you review each day's events at regular intervals. For example, if you wanted to remember the events on a particular Monday, not only would you run through them on Monday night, but also Tuesday night, the following Monday, then a month later and three months later. Doing this would ensure that the events of that Monday are fixed in your long-term memory.

You could, then, use this as a means of remembering your whole life. If you decide to do this, do it regularly. As with any other skill, the more you practise the better you will get. You can further ensure that you remember these events by combining this mental review with the keeping of a diary. Reviewing your diary entries at regular intervals will further enhance your recall.

Physical Performance
You can use visualisation to push your physical performance to a higher level. Suppose, for example, you are in the gym and you want to push yourself harder: you might want to lift a heavier weight than you have lifted before, or run a particular distance faster than you have done before. Use your powers of visualisation to see yourself achieving what you want to achieve. Make sure that you are fully emotionally involved in what you are doing: if you find getting angry helps you push yourself harder, then use your imagination to visualise something that makes you angry.

You can also practise physical skills using visualisation. If there is any particular skill that you want to develop or improve upon, remember that mental practice can be just as effective as physical practice, so set aside some time for mental review. Imagine yourself performing the activity with as much clarity as you can.

Achieving your goals
Your imagination has one major advantage over real life: you can *imagine* yourself doing things that you *can't* actually do or at least that you believe

you can't. Make a list of things that you haven't done yet but would like to do: maybe things that you have difficulty believing you are capable of.

Pick one item on the list and try to imagine what it would be like if you actually succeeded. Involve your senses fully and bring in all your emotions as well. See whether this changes how you feel about the activity, whether you feel more or less motivated to do it, and whether it changes your perceptions about what is possible.

Onword

In this section we have dealt in detail with developing and using your visualisation skills. In the following, we will deal with ways to help you develop each of your five senses further by giving you exercises that will enable you to focus on each one at a time.

Answers to auditory assessment exercise

"To be or not to be, *that is the question*", Hamlet;

"One for all, and *all for one*", the Three Musketeers;

"Yesterday, all my troubles *seemed so far away*", the Beatles;

"Our Father, Who art in Heaven, *Hallowed be Thy Name*", the Lord's Prayer.

FOUR

DEVELOPING YOUR SENSES

So far in this course we have been talking about the inner world. The aim of this section is to help you to develop a better awareness in all of your senses in relation to the outside world. You are going to practise really using each of your different senses in ways that you might not have done before, or at least since you were a child.

Developing your senses in this way will help you attain a greater appreciation of the outside world and undoubtedly enhance your quality of life. You will become more alert to what is going on around you. You will stimulate your brain, and ultimately this will help with your visualisation exercises, as it will give you a greater range of experiences to play with.

Materials for sense development exercises

You will need to obtain some items to practise on. Try to obtain as many of the following as you can: -

- Fresh fruit and vegetables: especially those that have a strong smell, such as oranges and lemons;

- Cheeses: go for a wide variety of smelly ones;

- Flowers: go for a wide variety with strong smells;

- Bread: again go for a variety of different loaves and make sure they are fresh.

The following exercises should be easy and fun to do. You are simply going to explore the items on the list as fully as you can by using your different senses. Try to make sure you do this with a sense of curiosity and fun. Set aside about twenty minutes to half an hour and gradually work your way through each exercise.

Your visual sense

Take one of the items and examine it visually. Look at it is if you were looking at it for the first time. Be particularly aware of the colour and shape of the object. Look at it from different angles and distances, as if you are an artist. Turn it over and look at it from upside down.

When you done this, close your eyes and try to reproduce the same experience completely. Try to capture the essence of the item in your mind's eye. When you have finished make a note of the experience.

Your sense of touch

Close your eyes and explore the various items using just your sense of touch. Feel the texture and shape of the various items. See if you can identify each different object with just your sense of touch. If you can't, take a look, and learn what the object feels like, so that you will know the next time. Squeeze the vegetables and fruit feel how hard or soft they are. Tear up some of the items. For instance, tear up the bread and really feel it as you do so. Notice how it feels different on the inside to the outside.

Now try to replicate what you have experienced in your imagination. Try to imagine as precisely as you can what each object feels like. Again, make a few notes when you have finished.

Your sense of smell

Take each of the items and smell them. Close your eyes so that you can really focus on the smell. Start off with the items with the most subtle aromas and then move on to the smellier ones. When you have done this a few times, have a go at identifying the various items solely by using your sense of smell. Smell is the sense which can most easily trigger memories and it is often the most underdeveloped, so developing your sense of smell will also help with developing your memory.

As before, when you have smelt each item, put it down and try to imagine what it smelt like. Again, make a few notes when you have finished.

Your sense of hearing

Take one of the vegetables or pieces of fruit and bite into it. Listen closely to the sound it makes. Feel, as well as hear, the sound as it travels through your jawbone to your ears, and listen closely to the sound of yourself chewing. Now take the orange and peel it. Listen very closely as the skin separates from the orange. Take one of the flowers and pull its stem apart. Listen to the sound it makes as you do so. Again, when you have done this, try to hear the sounds in your head.

Your sense of taste

Take one of the items of food and bite into it. Hold it in your mouth, and identify the different components of the taste – sweet and sour, salt and bitter. Notice where on your tongue and in your mouth these different elements are most prominent. When eating others foods, try and identify the different ingredients. Again, use your imagination to relive the experience.

Developing the senses without using sight

As you become more adept at these exercises, try to do them all with your eyes closed (except for the exercise to develop your visual sense). Make sure that you can always identify the item you are working with, using each of your different senses.

Continuing with the development of your senses

When you have exhausted the items on the list, go out and find some new ones to play with. Make sure that you choose items that can be explored with all the senses. Food and drink are ideal.

Also, make a decision to continue developing your senses in the world at large. When you look at an object really look at it. Try to gain as much visual information about it as you possibly can. Also, start to become aware of your peripheral vision. How much can you learn to see out of the corner of your eyes? Do the same for the other senses. Listen closely to the sounds around you all the time. Whenever you hear a piece of music on the radio, listen closely to it and try to identify all of the different instruments. When it has finished, try to hear it again in your head.

Do the same for smell touch and taste. When eating, focus on the taste, the smell and the texture of the food. Make sure that you can identify what you are eating with your eyes closed.

As your senses continue to develop, you might like to try a few exercises with a blindfold on. If you are feeling brave, try finding your way round your house. See how well you can find your way around without being able to see, using only your remaining four senses. This exercise will be a real test of how much they have developed. Obviously, if you are going to do this make sure that you are not likely to put yourself in a situation where you might get injured. Put away any dangerous objects and move

Visualisation

slowly enough so that if you bump into something you won't hurt yourself. Be particularly aware of any stairs in your building. Perhaps you could get someone to watch to ensure that you do not hurt yourself.

Incorporate all of the exercises in this section into your ongoing visualisation and make sure that you plan what you are going to do. As before you might find it useful to make a few notes at the end of each session to remind yourself how it went. Review these notes at regular intervals (and schedule some time for review in your planning), so that you can see how you are progressing.

Onword

We have now covered all of the substantive material on this Visualisation Course. In the following *Ongoing Practice* section we will provide you with strategies to enable you to continue developing your visualisation skills.

FIVE

ONGOING PRACTICE

In the early stages of your visualisation practice, try to ensure that you do the exercises every day for at least a month. Work through the different visualisation exercises we have included and when you have completed these either do them again or start to develop your own.

When a month has elapsed, assess what you have learnt and consider whether you want to continue. Write down what you think you have gained from doing these exercises and what benefits they have brought to you in your life. Write down anything else that occurs to you as well. Also note down what you think you will gain from continuing to do your concentration exercises and identify what would happen if you gave up. Use these notes as a source of motivation to continue with the exercises. We advise you to conduct a review of your progress every three months.

Ideally, you will want to incorporate visualisation exercises into your life an ongoing daily basis. If you do so the benefits to your long-term performance will be maximised. With these exercises, success is not just a goal, it is also the path itself, and part of that success is the discipline that comes with ongoing perseverance.

As we have already said, one of the greatest obstacles to progress with these exercises is impatience. You will initially notice large benefits, but gradually the law of diminishing returns will set in, and the benefits will become less noticeable. However, the long-term benefits are just as important even if they are less obvious. So make a decision to persevere.

Another danger is that you will acknowledge the benefits of the visualisation exercises but fail to make a committed decision to do the exercises regularly. In this case, you will obtain some benefit, but will not maximize the benefits that you might get. The rest of this section is aimed at helping you persist with your exercises.

Time of day

In the initial stages you might like to experiment with practising at different times of day. However, when you have identified the time of day that suits you best, try and stick with it. For most people the best times are either immediately after waking up or just before going to bed. If you choose the latter make sure you do not fall asleep while doing your exercises.

By doing the same thing at the same time, you are establishing new neural pathways that your brain will automatically follow – in other words you will form a new, positive, habit.

How long?

You should spend about twenty minutes at a time performing your visualisation exercises. If you cannot spare twenty minutes, try and do whatever you can, but consider rescheduling your other commitments. In the long run the benefits of spending twenty minutes a day doing these exercises will outweigh the costs. Try always to focus on the longer-term benefits. Most people's problems, difficulties and challenges usually spring from having a focus that is too short term.

If you have more time available, try to do two twenty-minute sessions a day, one in the morning, one in the evening. Doing two sessions a day will improve your long term ability to visualise. Alternatively, if you only have time to do one session, try and extend that session, aiming to increase it to forty minutes a day if you can. However, if you do not have the extra time, one twenty-minute session per day is perfectly acceptable.

Planning

An excellent way of making sure that you continue with your exercises is to plan them before you do them. Furthermore, if your plans are in writing you are more likely to put them into practice.

The best time to do your planning is the night before, so that when you do are planning you are not distracted by the events of the following day. This makes it easier to be firm about what you are going to do.

When planning, focus on the following factors: -

- The seven visualisation exercises on this course

- Developing your own visualisation exercises

- Using visualisation to enhance your memory

- Using visualisation to enhance you physical performance

- Using visualisation to achieve your goals

- Developing your senses

- The exercise, *'assessing your powers of visualisation'* on page 17 (repeat this after three months to see how your abilities are improving).

Combining the Visualisation Course with our Concentration & Focus Short Course

We suggest that, if you have not already done so, you move on to the *Concentration & Focus Course*. These two courses are closely related to each in that they both make use of the same state of mind, but with different goals.

If you are interested in using the *Concentration & Focus Course* while continuing with the *Visualisation Course*, you will need to work out a way of combining them that works for you. You might try doing concentration exercises on one day and visualisation on the following, or one in the morning and the other in the evening, or one immediately after the other. Again, experiment and find out what works best for you.

SIX

ENDWORD

You have now completed the *Visualisation Short Course*. You might now wish to consider other areas of mental, cognitive and intellectual development. If so, information about our other courses, books and other products can be found on our website www.oxfordmind.co.uk

VISUALISATION MATERIALS

1. Home visualisation

Stand outside your house and look at it. What does it look like? What colour is the front door. How many windows can you see? Look at them closely? What are the window surrounds made of? What can you see through them? Can you see into the rooms or are there curtains or blinds?

What noises can you hear outside? Can you hear traffic, or people walking by? Can you smell anything? If you have a garden what flowers can you see? Can you smell them? Are there any animals in the garden? Walk up to the front door. Put your hand on it and feel it. What does it feel like? What sort of handle does it have? Feel the handle. Open the door slowly. Does it make any noise? Is it light or heavy? Does it open to the left or the right?

Walk inside. Look at the floor. Is there carpet on the floor, wood or something else? Imagine that your feet are bare. How does it feel underfoot? Is the carpet lush or ragged? Is the wood smooth or rough? Look around at the walls. What can you see? Are they plain or patterned? Is there anything on them? What can you hear? Is there music playing? Can you hear other people? Do you see anyone? What are they wearing?

Think about the locations of the different rooms in the house? Where is the kitchen? The bedrooms? The bathrooms? The living room? Are there many rooms or only a few? Walk around the house in your mind going into each room? As you do so notice how the sounds change as you do so.

Do any of the floors make a noise as you walk on them? Feel the walls and the doors as you go into each room? How do they differ from room to room? Do the colours change as you walk around the house? Are some rooms brighter than others? What about the furniture? What does it look like? Is it hard or soft? Plain or patterned? Sit in the different chairs around the house? Which are the most comfortable? Which do you like most and which do you like least?

Pick up the different objects in the different rooms. Weigh them in your hands. Move them around. Go to your bedroom and lie on the bed. How does it feel? Try lying upside down on the bed. How does that change your perspective? If you have other bedrooms go in there and do the same thing. How does that feel? Does it feel different?

As you wander round the house be aware of any smells. What can you smell in the kitchen? Can you smell food? Go to the fridge and see what is in there? Take out whatever you see and taste it?

Do you have any pets? Are there animal smells anywhere? Go and say hello to them?

Do you have a back garden? Go outside into it? How did you get outside? What can you see in the garden? Is it grassed or paved? Are there plants, flowers or trees? Are there any garden ornaments?

What is the weather like? Is it sunny or cloudy? Hot or cold? Is it raining? Snowing? Can you smell any outdoor smells? Flowers? Animals? What sounds can you hear? Are there country sounds or city sounds? Can you hear animals? Traffic? Are there aeroplanes overhead? Walk around the garden and explore it. Notice all the different sights and sounds and smells.

When you have finished exploring the garden, gradually bring your attention back to the outside world to conclude this session.

2. Mountain trip

Visualise yourself in a grassy meadow at the base of a mountain. Look up and see the cone-like shape of the mountain as it towers above you, snow covering its peak. Look around the meadow. Do you see the grass? Flowers? Can you smell them? Are there any animals? Listen to the sounds they make? Can you hear the birds singing as they fly around and over you? Feel the sun on your body and a gentle breeze on your skin.

Slowly walk toward the mountain along a gentle path. Eventually you come to a small stream which you have to cross. Listen to the water as it gurgles and splashes on its way. Bend down and scoop up a handful of water in your cupped hands. It is freezing cold. Take a cooling sip and then let the rest slip away between your fingers.

Carry on the path up the mountain. The path is gentle, not too steep. You feel the exertion, you have broken out into a gentle sweat, your breathing is a little harder and your heart is pumping. Feel it. As you carry on up the path to the top you see a pond. The water is still as glass. Take off your clothes, jump in the pond and go for a swim. In this fantasy you can swim, even if normally you cannot. Feel the water as it flows around your body. Feel the sun beating down on you. When you have finished swimming get out of the pond and let the sun dry the water on your body. It feels fantastic.

Put your clothes back on and carry on up the mountain. You are now more than half way up. Look back down behind you. You can see a large valley and the meadow where you started off. Look up. See the birds flying around and making their nests in the cliffs. Listen to the birdsong.

You are now getting towards the top. There is snow underfoot. Listen to the sound it makes under your boots as you take each step. Bend down, scoop up a handful. Fashion it into a snowball and throw it as far as you can back down the mountain.

You are now at the top. It is time to take a rest and admire the view. Take some deep breaths and breathe in the pure mountain air. Listen to the sound of silence.

When you are ready start back down the mountain. Feel the force of gravity as it helps you take large bouncy steps down the mountainside. As you look up you see the sun setting. The sky is a beautiful rich shade of red. Pass the pond, and the stream to find yourself back in the meadow from where you started off. Lie down in the meadow and relax.

Gradually bring your attention back to the outside world to conclude this session.

3. Beach visualisation

Imagine that you are alone on a beautiful, sunny beach. The sun is beating down on you from above. It is hot but not uncomfortable. The sand is very dry, fine and almost white. Feel it under foot. Feel it between your toes. It is lovely and warm. Now run down to the shoreline. The sand is wet here.

Feel how it changes underfoot. Bend down and stick your hands in the sand, like a child, and feel it. It is wet and clay-like. Rub it between your fingers and thumbs. Now stand up and look at the sea. It is blue and it is beautiful, extending off into the distance as far as the eye can see. Breathe in deeply and smell the salty sea air. You can almost taste it. You hear a gull crying as it flies overhead.

You decide to take a swim. Run into the sea. You can swim in this fantasy even if normally you cannot. The water is cool against your skin. Feel it. When it is deep enough you take your feet off the bottom and swim. The water easily supports your weight. Feel it splash around your head. Feel the taste of the salty water as it splashes round your mouth and nose.

Now take a deep breath and dive underwater. As you dive down a whole new world is revealed to you. You can see hundreds of fish of all different types swimming round in the sea with you. There are as many different colours as you can imagine. Some are large, some are small. Some beautiful, some ugly and grotesque. Some swim in shoals hundreds strong; some are solitary. On the bottom you can see starfish, seahorses and what looks like millions of shells.

You see a large oyster shell on the bottom. Swim down to it and open it up. Inside is the most magnificent pearl. Take it out, swim back to the surface, and gently return to the beach. When you are back on dry land look at the pearl. Admire its opaque colour. Feel it. Roll it between your finger and thumb. Now slowly walk back up the beach. Find your towel and lie down, letting the sun cool you off.

Gradually bring your attention back to the outside world to conclude this session.

4. Hiking visualisation

You are going for a hike. You have just left a country road, and are crossing a field towards some woods. As you approach the wood you can see that it is a pine wood. Before long you can smell it as well. It smells so fresh. It is warm, but there are some clouds in the sky, and it starts to rain lightly. The sun is still shining though and the rain is welcome and refreshing. As it rains you can see a rainbow in the sky in front of you.

You are now entering the woods. The air is cooler as you are in the shade. There is a path guiding you through the wood. It is covered in small twigs, which crack and crunch underfoot as you walk along. As you walk, taking in the lovely pine smell, a sharp movement catches the corner of your eye. You follow the movement to see a squirrel running up a tree. You stop and watch it for a few moments.

You carry on along the path. There is another animal on the path in front of you. It is a small deer. It is not afraid of you, and slowly you walk up to it, your hand outstretched. It nuzzles your hand. Its nose is cold and wet. You stroke the soft fur on its neck. It is silky smooth. Enjoy this moment of connection. After a while the deer runs off into the depths of the forest. You try and listen to it running for as long as you can but eventually the sound disappears.

You carry on along the path for a few more minutes. Then you come into a clearing with a small lake. On the other side someone is swimming. You can see them but they can't see you. You watch them as they slowly get out on the other side of the lake and get dressed. You are utterly entranced, for this person is stunningly beautiful. You finally manage to tear yourself away and carry on along the path. After a few more minutes walking you come to the edge of the forest and decide to stop for a rest.

Enjoy this rest for as long as you wish and when you are ready gradually bring your attention back to the outside world.

5. Baby visualisation

Imagine that you are a baby of about fifteen months old. Everything in the world is still new and exciting. You are in your favourite room, playing with your favourite toy. What is it? Look at it. Feel it. What does it smell like? Can you stick it in your mouth? What would that feel like? You are totally engrossed in what you are doing. Nothing could distract you. Just enjoy playing with it for a few minutes.

You look up and notice that your parents are watching you. There are smiles on their faces and they are enjoying your happiness. You feel warm and safe. Everything you could possibly want in the world is here with you.

Enjoy this fantasy for as long as you wish and when you are ready gradually bring your attention back to the outside world.

6. Picnic fantasy

Imagine you are going on a picnic in the countryside. The love of your life is with you, and you are both relaxing, lying on a blanket. In the picnic hamper beside you is a wonderful array of your favourite foods and drinks. The smell is intoxicating. Take some of the food out of the hamper. You can hardly wait to try it, it smells so good. You already have a mouthful of saliva in anticipation of the taste. Put some food in your mouth. How does it taste. Let the taste engulf your mouth. Carry on with this sumptuous feast. Enjoy it. There is no hurry. This is the best picnic ever.

You look around. There are cows and sheep in the field with you chomping away on the grass. Clouds gently scud across the sky and the occasional bird flies by. Way up in the sky you can see a large jet flying away, carving out a vapour trail in the sky.

Enjoy this fantasy for as long as you want, noticing what is going on around you. When you are ready bring your attention back to the outside world.

7. Water visualisation

Visualise a glass of water in front of you. How big is it? Is it small or large? What colour is the glass? Is it plain or coloured? What texture is the glass? Do you see the glass standing on something or is it floating in the air in front of you? Pick it up. Is it light or is it heavy? Does it fill your hand? How much water is in it? How dry does your mouth feel? Do you need a drink? Take a sip of water. Do you have to tilt the glass a lot or a little? How does your mouth feel now? What temperature is the water? Cold, freezing cold, lukewarm, warm or hot? Is it pleasant? Swill the water around in your mouth and then swallow it.

Now imagine the remaining water in the glass turning into wine? Is it red or white? Has the glass changed into a wine glass or has it stayed the same? Swirl the wine around. How does that feel? Now take a smell. What does it smell like? Lift the glass to your lips and take a sip. What does it taste like? Feel the wine on your tongue. Which bits of your tongue are stimulated? Is the wine warm or cold? Swallow the wine and notice the feelings as it travels down your throat to your stomach? Can you feel it settling on your stomach?

Now imagine the glass of water again. Watch as the glass of water floats slowly up into the air in front of you. Rotate the glass slowly in your mind so that it is upside down, but notice that the water stays in the glass. Now make the glass bigger in your mind? Now make it smaller. Now return it to its former size.

Turn the glass back to the right way up. Change the colour of the water. Make it blue. Now make it red. And now green. And now yellow. Does changing the colour affect anything else? Are there any different smells? What does yellow water smell like?

Visualisation

Now turn the glass over again and let the water fall out of the glass and splash onto the floor. What sound does it make? Now let the glass drop to the floor and watch it smash. Listen to the sound as the glass smashes.

Now something very strange happens. Time starts running backwards. Watch the scene in reverse. Watch the shards of glass that are scattered all over the floor collect themselves together and reform the glass. Watch as it rises back into the air and watch the water jump back into it from the floor. When the glass is full again turn it back the right way up and then put it down on a table in front of you.

When you have done so, gradually bring your attention back to the outside world to conclude this session.

More Short Courses Coming Soon!

Analytical Thinking

Creative Thinking

Setting and Achieving Goals

Powerful States of Mind

Essential Communication Skills

Emulating Success

Healthy Eating

Healthy Sleep

Printed in Poland
by Amazon Fulfillment
Poland Sp. z o.o., Wrocław